TEXAS
A&M
UNIVERSITY

*"…men from the farm, the shop, the counter,
the bench, the senate and the forum, who have been
prepared for life's great struggle here, will…
in poetry and song, and in silvery eloquence,
chant the praises of their Alma Mater."*

Governor Richard Coke
Dedication Ceremony, 1876
Agricultural & Mechanical College of Texas

TEXAS A&M
UNIVERSITY

A LEGACY *of* TRADITION

 osso

NANCY GLENN

PHOTOGRAPHY BY BOB HERGER

To Zach '06
May this book
be a cherished reminder
of Texas A & M.
Gig 'Em!
Nancy Glenn
September 6, 2003

This book is dedicated to Barry,
Carrie, and Kim for their encouragement,
support, and steadfast love.

TEXAS A&M UNIVERSITY
A Legacy of Tradition

FIRST EDITION 1999
Text and Photography Copyright © 1999 Spectrum Fine Arts Publishing

Written and Compiled by Nancy Glenn
Photography by Bob Herger (except as noted)
Design by Kelly Brooks
Edited by Tina L. Evans
Production Consulting and Photo Editing by David O. Cooper

Copyright © 1999 Spectrum Fine Arts Publishing
P.O. Box 10795, College Station, Texas 77842
First Printing, 1999   Printed in the United States of America

ISBN 0-9667648-0-3

THE INDICIA DEPICTED ON THIS PRODUCT
ARE TRADEMARKS OF TEXAS A&M UNIVERSITY

❧ CONTENTS ❧

❧ P REFACE ❧

ONCE, THERE WAS ONLY THE PRAIRIE—immense, windswept, strewn with brush and bluebonnet. What vision it must have taken to imagine, on that spot, one of the world's great universities: a place of wisdom, tradition, and a sense of spirit so profound that it lives forever in the hearts of its former students.

In this collection of photographs, I have endeavored to create an enduring portrait of the character and spirit that are so much a part of this place. With photographer Bob Herger, I enjoyed capturing visual expressions of the dignity, grace, and awesome beauty of the area. I am deeply grateful for Bob's talent, expertise, and sensitive eye.

I also wish to thank Maj. Gen. M.T. "Ted" Hopgood, Jr., Maj. Greg Johnson, Maj. Gen. Thomas Darling, Lt. Col. Jim Harrison, Lt. Col. Jay Brewer, Lt. Col. Keith Stephens, Lt. Col. Jake Betty, Pat and Joe Fenton, and the many outstanding young men and women of the Corps of Cadets for responding so warmly and generously to all my requests. The staff at the campus art galleries, including Tim Novak, Catherine Hastedt, and Lalaine Little, have been so helpful. The gracious staff at the Cushing Memorial Library, including Donald Dyal, David Chapman, Steve Smith, and Angus Martin, have enlightened and inspired me.

I want to offer warm thanks to Charles Hermann, Director of the Bush School; the helpful staff at the Bush Presidential Library Complex, especially Don Wilson and David Alsobrook; Ann Black and the OPAS staff; Wally Groff and other helpful staff in the Athletic Department; Tim Donathen of the

Facilities Department; Nancy W. Dickey, M.D., of the College of Medicine; and Robert Wegener and the staff at the *Battalion* newspaper.

I would also like to thank many others who have generously offered their friendship and wise counsel, including Jerry Cooper, Henry Dethloff, Margaret Rudder, Sanders Letbetter, Toby Boenig, and artist Ivana Candiago.

A number of people have been so very kind by offering their invaluable expertise, support, and friendship during this project, including Tina Evans, David Cooper, Karen Cooper, Kelly Brooks, Carol Kerns, Ann Rife, and Margaret and Chris Segrest. To everyone who has helped along the way, I thank you.

❧

Here in this valley, the land is graced with timeless natural beauty; and in the halls of our great University, the wisdom of leaders past and present will live forever. For those who know this extraordinary place, my hope is that these words and images will renew our sense of wonder. For others, I hope they will be an inspiration.

Texas A&M and the Brazos Valley community are happy to welcome visitors. We know that you, too, will be moved by the beauty, character, and history that have shaped the place we call home. We hope you will also come away with a sense of what makes this place so very special.

Nancy Glenn

❧ INTRODUCTION ❧

Since its dedication in 1876, Texas A&M University has enjoyed a vigorous and committed student community. Today, the University is revered and loved by its former and present students, and by many who look forward to attending. Here patriotism, pride, and the natural beauty of the Brazos Valley converge among structures and statues that memorialize a long and vibrant history—the legacy of A&M. It is this legacy that inspires those who come generations later to reach for what is good, true, and noble. Within these walls, where honor is prized and a passion for knowledge burns brightly, the immutable values of generations past continue to shape the future.

These are the values that underlie Texas A&M University, whose campus reflects its history, and whose students reflect its future. Against this backdrop, each of us paints his own personal experience; perhaps these photographs will inspire your own dreams and memories. I hope this book will help those who have experienced Texas A&M to relive it, those who reside here to see the campus with new eyes, and those who are strangers to it to share in something extraordinary.

At Texas A&M, the past is ever-present—guiding, inspiring, and lighting the way. Just as much a source of pride, however, are the ongoing achievements of the University and its present students. A&M is widely known for its commitment to the integration of research and teaching, which allows students to experience the excitement of discovery. Research expenditures at Texas A&M place the University among the nation's Top Ten research universities as ranked by the National Science Foundation. The cutting-edge technology and creative activity that emerge from Texas A&M benefit not only the people of Texas, but also the nation and the world.

Texas A&M encourages a sense of community through the largest student-union program in America: approximately 650 clubs and organizations are recognized by the University and its Memorial Student Center. This wide-ranging support of social, recreational, and personal development interests is recognized as a vital part of an A&M education—a context within which individual character is shaped.

෴

I have lived in the Brazos Valley for many years, and I have never ceased to be amazed by the majesty of Texas A&M, the honor of the faculty and students, and the character of the people in this community. My love for this area has only increased with time.

The splendor of a sunrise, the exuberance of wildflowers, the grace of art and architecture...a heritage rich in honor, a stadium brimming with impassioned fans...all inspire pride in the great State of Texas and Texas A&M University. Things of physical beauty draw people to this place, but it is the element of spiritual beauty that affects us most deeply. The University was founded on a core belief in personal honor and integrity—principles that have contributed to a unique blend of tradition, education, and camaraderie. A&M is more than the buildings its founders and leaders have left behind; it is the legacy of character that has made this University great.

The jewel-like hues of early morning
illuminate the Memorial Student Center
and the impressive Rudder Tower,
home of a theater complex that sparkles
with exciting productions.

A FOUNDATION
for GREATNESS

There are moments in history when foundations are laid that will shape generations for centuries to come. Such moments are made possible by people of wisdom and foresight, who see beyond the realm of their own vision. In 1876, when the Agricultural & Mechanical College of Texas was dedicated on the site of what once had been a humble dewberry patch, its founding fathers must have envisioned a great future for the school. Perhaps they even dreamed it would one day become the world-class institution it is today— Texas A&M University.

From a lofty vantage point, one beholds a breathtaking view of the University and the Brazos Valley that is its home.

"An immense prairie, containing a
scattering of post oak trees...
had previously served as an assembly
point for cattle drives..."

*Deborah McWilliams Balliew '78
in her book, College Station Texas 1938/1988*

Like a glorious cloak, fog embraces the Jack K. Williams Administration Building, named in honor of the University's 17th President.

*Literature and architecture converge
as a student loses herself
in verse near the building's
front promenade.*

"All things considered, the administration
building is by far the most grandiosely
conceived structure ever erected on the
campus of Texas A&M College."

*Ernest Langford '13
in his manuscript, Here We'll Build the College, 1963*

A quiet stillness falls over the Administration Building,
which stands majestically at the University's main entrance.

Robed figures bring the poetic grace of
classical beauty to the flagpole's pedestal.

"One hundred stonemasons, mostly Italian, worked every
week for one year to make the Administration Building
one of the most beautiful in the State."

Pat Morley
referring to the ornamental stonework, 1983

*An impressive colonnade adds
grandeur to the Administration Building's facade.*

The Administration Building's main lobby is an architectural triumph, from massive fluted columns to the exquisite detail of a bas-relief ceiling panel haloed in light.

"Sentimentalists have for ages endowed old buildings with voices which speak of times past."

Ernest Langford '13
in his manuscript, Here We'll Build the College, 1963

In striking visual contrast to the vintage architecture of the Administration Building is the 15-story Eller Oceanography and Meteorology Building, a sweeping limestone structure topped by a weather observation laboratory.

Shrouded in the morning mist,
towering oaks bring majestic
beauty to the University's main
entrance and beyond.

"I think I shall like it."

Lawrence Sullivan Ross
in a letter to a friend written his first day
as President of A&M College of Texas
February 2, 1891

The campus is silent in the misty
hours of early dawn, as a couple
shares a tranquil moment.

*The fog of early morning
lifts to reveal a profusion of
vibrant color.*

*"The grounds I found adapted to the purpose
almost as if designed by nature, or prescribed
by a most skillful connoisseur."*

C.G. Forshey
first architect, A&M College of Texas, 1871
History of the Agricultural and Mechanical College of Texas, 1935

"We should form and ever preserve an organization for uniting us fraternally, and always at necessity's call, extend a helping hand to an old comrade."

*an objective of The Association of Ex-Cadets
(forerunner of The Association of Former Students), 1879*

The crescent-shaped home of The Association of Former Students takes on a mystical, resplendent beauty in the first rays of dawn. The largest stand-alone alumni center in the nation is named for Clayton W. Williams, Jr. '54.

*Foxgloves flourish in the floral test
gardens just past the
Alumni Center's Great Hall.*

"...to perpetuate the ties of friendships formed during college days..."

James "Randy" Matson '67
on the missions of The Association of Former Students

Light and shadow define the
Center and its exceptional passive-flow
fountain, dedicated by three Aggie sons
to the memory of their father and
in honor of their mother.

*The graceful bluebonnet,
State Flower of Texas, carpets the
surrounding landscape and offers a
vivid setting for a couple's
magnificent Aggie Senior Rings.*

"The Texas A&M senior ring is a tradition as grand as the University itself... symbolic of hard work and of membership in the greatest fellowship in the world."

*Cadence
December 1997*

*The Armillary Sphere sundial reaches
skyward to catch the radiant sun
glinting through afternoon clouds.*

A brocade of spring blossoms
gently graces the elegant,
colonnaded entrance to the home
of the University President.

"Earl and I have so many fond memories of our time in the President's Home. We feel extremely honored to have been the first family to live in such a lovely place."

Margaret Rudder
wife of the late Maj. Gen. James Earl Rudder '32

*A sapphire sky forms the backdrop for the
Sam Houston Sanders Corps of Cadets Center
and museum as it presides over the heritage
and spirit of Aggieland.*

A HISTORY
of TRADITION

*I*t inspires. It enlightens. There's
nothing like it anywhere else: the Aggie
Spirit. However intangible and difficult
to define, it is very real in the hearts of
Aggies, and it is deeply steeped in
tradition. At the heart of A&M lies the
Corps of Cadets, which originated
many of the traditions that remain an
integral part of the University today—
traditions that form the basis of a lifelong
bond among Aggies all over the world.

A heritage to treasure —
military boots and hat worn by
Fred W. Dollar '44 as a member
of Third Headquarters Battery,
Horse-drawn Field Artillery.

A centerpiece of respect and honor —
a diorama prominently displays the
uniforms of Aggieland.

"Being a guard member is not only a privilege but
also an honor. It is our responsibility to maintain
and pass on the pride and spirit of being an Aggie
to the many people who visit A&M each year."

Philip A. Gomez '99
Corps Center Guard Commander

Yell Leader and sports memorabilia
proudly recall the early days of
A&M Athletics.

*"Yell practice...fine, moving occasions long
remembered in hearts of Aggies."*

Cadence
December 1997

*An A&M football helmet rests on a Southwest
Conference Championship banner from 1956.
1957 Heisman Trophy winner John David
Crow '58 is featured in the photograph.*

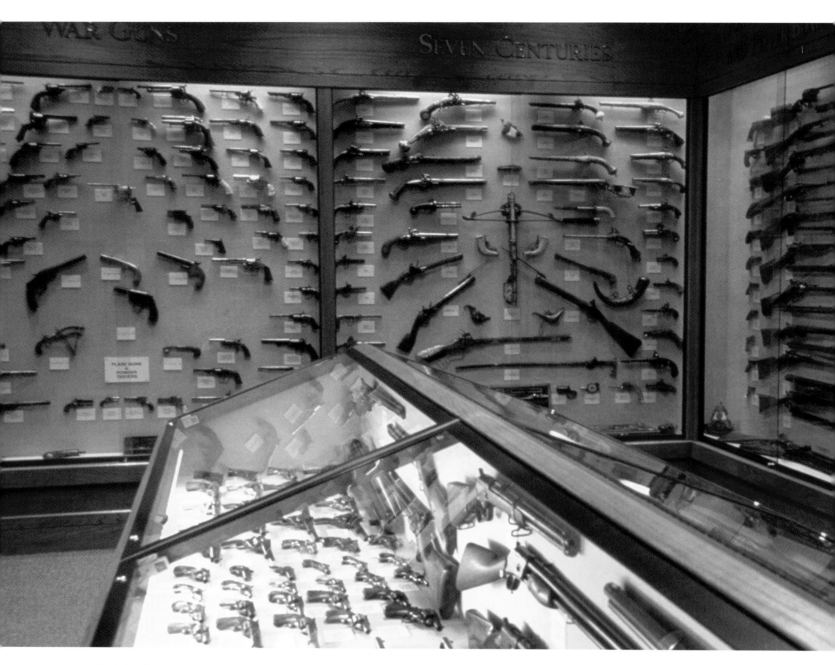

*Symbols of freedom—over 600 rare
and valuable firearms and accessories
comprise the priceless Sanders-Metzger
Gun Collection in the Corps Center.*

*"The greatest prize of any Colt Collection is the 1847
Colt Walker carried by the Texas Rangers...designed
by Colonel Colt and Captain Walker."*

*Joe Fenton '58
Curator, Corps Center*

Forty-six proud stars — it is said this flag traveled with Teddy Roosevelt and his legendary Rough Riders.

The 1847 Colt Walker, displayed with powder flask, is one of fewer than one hundred survivors.

A lone oak in the stillness of morning lends a sense of uncommon calm to Kyle Field, the home of Aggie football.

*"There's a spirit can ne'er be told;
it's the spirit of Aggieland."*

*The Spirit of Aggieland,
the Texas A&M alma mater;
lyrics by Marvin H. Mimms '26*

Readiness, desire, and enthusiasm —
the tradition of the 12th Man was born
when E. King Gill left the stands to suit up,
just in case Coach needed him.
Gill's resolve inspired those of his own time
and challenges us still.

"I'll be in the stands if you need me."

E. King Gill '24
according to popular legend
January 2, 1922

WELCOME TO AGGIELAND

HOME OF THE 12TH MAN

Gill's readiness to serve kindled a flame of devotion
among the Aggie student body. As today's 12th Man,
Aggies stand throughout every A&M football game to
demonstrate that they are ready for duty if called.

*Aggie Yell Leaders "squeeze" during a
field goal to make sure the football
goes through the uprights.*

"Not only did I receive a quality education and play for Coach Bryant, but I became an Aggie. Not just for four years, but for a lifetime."

John David Crow '58
1957 Heisman Trophy Winner
on coach Paul "Bear" Bryant and Texas A&M

Johnson Photography

The nationally-renowned "Wrecking Crew"
defense has built a reputation for
stifling some of the most potent offenses
in collegiate football.

*Senior buglers stand motionless, awaiting
the Drum Major's command to lead
off another stirring performance of the
Fightin' Texas Aggie Band.*

TAMU Photo Imaging Services

Barker Productions

An impressive display of precision by the world's largest military marching band — the "Pulse of Aggieland."

"Ladies and gentlemen, now forming at the north end of Kyle Field, the nationally famous Fightin' Texas Aggie Band!"

Lt. Col. Jay O. Brewer '81
the voice of the Fightin' Texas Aggie Band

*Building the 65-foot Bonfire is a
remarkable feat of engineering.
Depicted here in bronze are
students "swamping" a log.*

---

*Members of the Corps and student
body spend hundreds of hours in
constructing the giant stack.*

"You hold the torch; see that it burns brightly
while in your hands..."

*Maj. Gen. M.T. "Ted" Hopgood, Jr. '65
Commandant, Corps of Cadets
addressing Corps members in "Aggie Reflections"*

A beacon in the night sky at "dark-thirty," Bonfire brings
together thousands of spirited Aggies, young and old,
to celebrate their "burning desire to beat t.u."

To the north of the Corps Center
stands the bronze Centennial Eagle,
a gift from the Class of 1976,
which honors a century of excellence
at Texas A&M.

*"Since 1876, the Corps has produced
individuals of strength and character
who refuse to accept defeat."*

Joe Fenton '58
Curator, Corps Center

The magnificent nine-foot Victory
Eagle sculpture and fountain, gifts
of the Class of 1991, are splendid
reflections of strength, courage,
and achievement.

At ease with his mount, a cadet pauses
moments before riding in formation
with the Parsons Mounted Cavalry.

*Passing on their leggings to junior
cadets, A&M Seniors are proud to
step into their coveted Senior Boots.*

*"As I prepared to pull on my Senior Boots and
handed Mike the leggings that had been passed down
to me, a million memories rushed through my
mind...all I had learned and the lifelong friends
I had made in the Cavalry."*

*Charles Gaitz '99
member, Parsons Mounted Cavalry*

"As any Texan knows, we all have a fierce pride in our great State. The only place that I can think of where this same pride is more acute is within the Texas borders, at her own Texas A&M University."

Greg Mabry, Class of 2000
member, Parsons Mounted Cavalry

Bugler for the Cavalry —
an honor bestowed on only
one cadet each year.

Both the Cavalry and the State of Texas bear proud symbols of tradition—cadets carefully tend the flag of the Lone Star State.

The Corps' Ross Volunteers are
the official Honor Guard for the
Governor of Texas. Their precision
drills are awe-inspiring.

The Ross Volunteers conduct a review during Parents Weekend. Members of the elite organization include many of the Corps' most outstanding upperclassmen.

"I am always willing to go above and beyond my best to uphold the motto of the Company: Soldier, Statesman, and Knightly Gentleman."

Joel Taylor '98
2nd Platoon Commander, Ross Volunteers

The noble Reveille, beloved collie mascot and
highest-ranking member of the Corps of Cadets,
with her Mascot Corporal in a moment of regal repose.

"A symbol of this University that
epitomizes the Aggie spirit and
tradition...she is the First Lady
of Texas A&M."

Craig Serold, Class of 2001
Mascot Corporal

A familiar face on campus, "Rev" is affectionately greeted
by all Corps fish (freshmen) with "Howdy, Miss Reveille, Ma'am."
Every year, a Mascot Corporal from the Corps' Company E-2 is given
the awesome responsibility and privilege of her day-to-day care.

*Members of Company E-2
lovingly tend the graves of Reveille I,
who died in 1944,
and of those who have followed her
in faithful service.*

"We'll think of one we'll ne'er more see,
our darling little Reveille."

John Ashton '06
Good-Bye, Reveille, a Tribute, 1944

They shall be honored and
remembered always — fresh flowers
adorn the gravesites of the beloved
A&M mascots for every home football
game and other special occasions.

TAMU Photo/Imaging Services

*Not a sound is heard but for the taps of
their steps in perfect unison —
the Corps' Ross Volunteers prepare
to perform their 21-gun salute at Muster.*

A solemn, moving ceremony —
a student honors a deceased
Aggie comrade during Muster,
a longtime A&M tradition.

"When I am finally alone in the shadow
of my days, I'll hear a Mustering of Aggies
and the echo of my name."

Randy Hester '74
Former Student

Dewdrops grace delicate roses and
a decorative star near the entrance
of the Administration Building.

*"Let your watchword be duty...
let honor be your guiding star."*

Governor Richard Coke
Dedication Ceremony, 1876
A&M College of Texas

Final Review is a bittersweet goodbye —
Seniors give their final salute as
members of the Corps, and watch as the
new officers assume their command.

The Flag Room in the Memorial
Student Center is a focal point and
traditional gathering place for Aggies.
The Center was dedicated in 1951
to "men of A&M who gave their lives
in defense of our country."

AN ARTISAN'S EYE
for BEAUTY

Texas A&M's commitment to

excellence includes an unwavering belief

that a broad-based, practical education

in the sciences and the arts is vital to all

its students. The University is dedicated

to providing a progressive environment

that fosters an appreciation for the fine

arts as pleasures to be enjoyed throughout

a lifetime. The art treasures that grace

the A&M campus encourage an enlight-

ened understanding of human expression

and stand as icons of enduring beauty.

*In the Memorial Student Center,
exquisite hand-carved wooden panels
reflect the University's first century.
Prominently featured is Tent Row,
makeshift housing that was first
erected in 1906 to serve an
overflowing student population.
The tents were used as needed for
almost two decades.*

The painstaking detail in the work of
Rodney and Sue Hill is a tribute to
the University and to those who
helped shape its destiny.

"In time tents were replaced by wooden shacks
about twenty feet square and 'Tent Row' became
'Hollywood'—a 'community' which ultimately
gave way to Law and Puryear Halls."

Ernest Langford '13
in his manuscript, Here We'll Build the College, 1963

Rudder Tower and its theater complex are reminders
of the friendly partnership between
the University and the local community.

*On his way to a morning class, a
Senior cadet passes beneath the
bronze statue of James Earl Rudder.*

"Earl Rudder was architect of the dream that
produced this center. In this, as in all he did,
he demonstrated uncommon ability to inspire
men and lead them to exceptional achievement."

Inscription on Rudder Tower

*Pausing to remember—a cadet views
medals from the distinguished
military career of Gen. James Earl
Rudder '32 in the impressive theater
complex named in his honor.*

*"Texas A&M was his favorite place in the
whole world, a place he really loved."*

*Margaret Rudder
on her husband, the late
Maj. Gen. James Earl Rudder '32*

A performance of elegance, poise, and grace by The Russian National Ballet beautifully represents the world-renowned productions brought to Rudder Auditorium by the Memorial Student Center Opera and Performing Arts Society.

From Broadway to opera, magnificent performances come to life onstage each season at Texas A&M.

A wealth of art in an extraordinary
setting—the MSC Forsyth Center
Galleries feature treasures by such
artists as Mary Cassatt, perhaps
America's best-loved Impressionist.

Plaque, Floralia
English Cameo Glass, white on plum
13 3/16" diameter
George Woodall (artist)
Thomas Webb & Sons (manufacturer)
988.1.106

Vase, two-handled
English Cameo Glass,
white on blue 15 3/8" height
George Woodall (artist)
Thomas Webb & Sons (manufacturer)
988.1.80

"...to provide students at Texas A&M University with an environment enriched by opportunities to enjoy important works of art."

Resolution of the Board of Regents
Texas A&M University System, 1986
in honor of J.W. "Bill" Runyon '35

Mary Cassatt
Mother in Large Hat Holding Her
Nude Baby, Seen in Back View
c.1909
oil on canvas
988.1.211

Frederic Remington
Modern Comanche
1890
oil on canvas
988.1.155

Works from the University's permanent
collection are presented on a rotating
basis by the Stark Galleries.

Traveling exhibits are featured in
the Stark Galleries' other two areas.
Showcased here is the Charles
Schorre Retrospective exhibit.

Among the outstanding temporary exhibits on display in the Memorial Student Center's Visual Arts Gallery is artist Ivana Candiago's Polyopsia exhibition.

"Good characteristics for painting for me are... outrageousness, mysteriously beautiful, unidentifiable elegance, always inventive and uniquely my own."

Charles Schorre
Artist
in the book, Charles Schorre, 1997

"You have a great privilege and opportunity, and I anticipate much pleasure in the use I know you will make of it."

*Col. E.B. Cushing, Class of 1880
encouraging a student to make
the most of his days at A&M
in a letter dated October 10, 1918*

David O. Cooper

*The Cushing Memorial Library is
marked by exceptional decoration
and architectural detail, including the
inscribed names of renowned scholars
such as Plato, Newton, Pasteur,
Watt, and Shakespeare.*

W.H. "Buck" Dunton
In Cattle Land
1912
Gift from the family of James L. Marr

The Cushing Memorial Library
holds many prized works
of art and literature.

Mᵣ WILLIAM
SHAKESPEARES
COMEDIES,
HISTORIES, and
TRAGEDIES.
Published according to the true Originall Copies.
The second Impression.

LONDON
Printed by Tho. Cotes, for William Aspley, and are to be sold at the signe
of the Parrot in Pauls Church-yard. 1632.

William Shakespeare
The Second Folio of Shakespeare
1632
Purchase made possible by
a gift from Chester J. Reed '47

Arnold Corrodi
*Luther's Explanation of the Bible
to Frederick of Saxony*
1873
Gift of C.C. "Polly" Krueger '12

*Standing as a memorial
to twelve former students who
were killed in World War II,
the Fish Pond fountain takes on
a soft glow in the evening hours.*

"Greater love hath no man than this,
that a man lay down his life for his friends."

John 15:13
The Holy Bible
bronze plaque, Memorial Student Center

Contemporary architecture and
design blend with the traditional in
the domed Academic Building and
surrounding structures—part of a
remarkable expansion that has
continued for over a century.

A RESPECT
for KNOWLEDGE

*T*he people of Texas A&M reflect

the honor, character, and forthrightness of

Texans everywhere. Stalwart in their efforts,

relentless in their purpose, and true in their

dedication, these are the individuals whose

contributions to the University are forever

a part of its greatness and its continuing

growth. Their forethought and wisdom have

established an enduring legacy—a University

that has educated, enlightened, and inspired

the many whose lives it has touched.

Built on the ashes of the Old Main building,
the Academic Building was completed in 1914
and remains to this day
one of the loveliest on campus.

The Silver Taps monument is a symbol of the
solemn Aggie ceremony held each month to remember
students who died while enrolled at A&M.
In their honor, the campus remains silent until morning.

*"There are times in the lives of men when...
the lips cannot give utterance to that which
the heart feeleth."*

The Honorable Norman G. Kittrell
at the memorial service for Lawrence Sullivan Ross
January 16, 1898

*Perhaps no image is more recognizable on campus
than that of Lawrence Sullivan Ross,
former Texas governor and beloved third president
of what was then the A&M College of Texas.*

"...he exhibited sterling common sense, lofty patriotism, inflexible
honesty, and, withal, a character so exalted that he commanded at
all times not only the confidence, but the affection of the people."

*Galveston Daily News
on Lawrence Sullivan Ross
January 4, 1898*

In the early days, it was said that parents
sent their sons to A&M just so they could be near
"Governor Ross," as he was loved and respected
by all who knew him.

Students often place coins
at the feet of "Sully"
for good luck on exams.

*Hallowed halls of learning —
looking skyward in the rotunda of the
Academic Building, one experiences a
dramatic view of a suspended
Liberty Bell replica.*

"*Where it is wrong, public opinion must be changed; where it is false, public sentiment must be corrected. We must begin at the fireside, keep it up in the school room, continue it in the press, urge it in the pulpit and complete it in the courts of justice.*"

*Lawrence Sullivan Ross
in his acceptance and inaugural address
as Governor of the State of Texas, 1887*

Elegant limestone arches at the base of the Albritton Bell Tower frame the Academic Building and beckon visitors to the main campus' west entrance.

Forty-nine bells ringing with pride and honor—the Westminster Carillon of the majestic Albritton Bell Tower peals in celebration of Aggie victories and tolls for Silver Taps.

The 138-foot Albritton Tower stands
as a beacon beyond R. Wofford
Cain Hall; to the north are the lights
of Bryan, whose citizens were
instrumental in the establishment
of the A&M College of Texas.

"I ring, I sing, I peal,
With a mighty force,
My love for God, family and country
And for that part of my heart
Which has never left
These hallowed halls."

Ford D. Albritton, Jr. '43
Inscription inside the tower

The spirit and dignity of a true Texas
rancher are captured in this bronze of
Robert Justus Kleberg, Jr., former
owner and director of the legendary
King Ranch, and his faithful mount.

A VISION
for the FUTURE

The courage to dream, to grow, to look beyond — these are hallmarks of the people of Texas A&M. Through their vision, the University continues to thrive and prosper, never resting on past accomplishments, but always striving toward an even greater fulfillment of promise. With the opening of a Presidential Library on its grounds, the University achieved a pinnacle in its growth as an educational institution and as a place of historical significance. It is indeed fortunate that today's University and its local communities are faithful friends and longtime partners in preserving their mutual legacy, and in ensuring that the area, its citizens, and its lands are blessed with a bright and prosperous future.

John J. Koldus Building

This structure at the very heart of campus honors John J. Koldus, who served twenty years as Vice President for Student Services. Koldus' dedication to A&M students is legendary.

"Henceforward, these halls are dedicated to the cause of liberal, scientific and practical education."

Governor Richard Coke
Dedication Ceremony, 1876
A&M College of Texas

With a dramatic sense of motion rare
in sculpture, this roughneck throws
a spinning chain to add a stem of pipe
to the drillstring.

*A&M's Student Recreation Center
is among the nation's premier
recreational sports facilities; nearby
Reed Arena is home to the A&M
basketball teams, the site of graduation
and campus Muster ceremonies, and a
popular venue for concerts and other
special events.*

"The outdoor exercise, the erect position and expanding
chest gives to the lungs the free play so essential after the
cramped position necessary to the school room..."

Governor Lawrence Sullivan Ross
in his letter accepting the presidency
of the A&M College of Texas, 1890

Sunlight gleams beyond the curve of a modern sculpture—symbolic of the hope that the physicians of tomorrow will bring to their patients.

The serenity of a parkbench setting surrounded by seasonal roses belies the flurry of classroom and research activity ever ongoing in the College of Medicine.

"A doctor touches mankind person by person, illness by illness, and each touch reflects on the families, the communities, the profession."

Nancy W. Dickey, M.D.
Associate Professor, College of Medicine
President, American Medical Association, 1998-99

Thanks to its location on a natural migratory fly-way,
the A&M campus is graced by a variety of
beautiful birds each season. The Mourning Dove at perch,
however, is a "resident bird," very much
at home in this campus setting.

"I will venture to hold a candle out to help light your path..."

Col. E.B. Cushing, Class of 1880
President of Alpha Phi fraternity
and the Alumni Association, forerunners
of the Association of Former Students
Letter to A&M student, 1918

Sunrise drenches the sky in glorious color far beyond the scoreboard of Kyle Field and the lights of the Clayton W. Williams, Jr. Alumni Center. The thriving city of College Station extends into the distance.

GEORGE BUSH LIBRARY

*An historic day in the life of Texas A&M —
the George Bush Presidential Library
and Museum was dedicated November 6, 1997.*

A wall of black granite
etched with the names of donors
leads the eye upward to a
rotunda fifty feet high at its peak.

"Character matters. Words are important,
but character is all that remains."

President George Bush
United States of America

"I want to teach and I still want to learn...
I want to share with the students
my thoughts on public service —
that service to a country is a calling."

President George Bush
United States of America

The George Bush School of Government and Public Service, located in the Presidential Library Complex, offers an exceptional learning environment. The school's master's program is geared for students interested in leading and managing organizations that serve the public interest.

A hush falls over the Presidential Library at nightfall, long after tourists and scholars have left its grounds and tranquil waters.

"Nothing can do a greater job today in fighting
the enemies of democracy than can the spirit,
the leadership, and the devotion to duty which
are so much a part of Texas A&M."

Maj. Gen. James Earl Rudder '32
Muster Address, 1956

Pages 10-11: The Memorial Student Center (MSC) was dedicated on Aggie Muster Day, April 21, 1951, in memory of former students who lost their lives during World War II. The MSC is a popular gathering place for students, and features a bookstore, several eateries, a hotel, meeting rooms, lounge areas, offices, a craft shop, a barber shop, and even a bowling alley.

In addition to housing the University's Faculty Club and a number of meeting rooms and executive offices (including that of the University President), Rudder Tower is home of the Leslie L. Appelt Aggieland Visitor Center, which offers campus tours, virtual tours of campus via computer terminals, and videotaped presentations highlighting the education, spirit, and history of Texas A&M. The Visitor Center is named after Leslie L. Appelt '41, who, through a generous gift, made the Visitor Center, its 9' x 12' videowall, and four interactive multimedia information kiosks possible. The 12-minute *Inspiration to Greatness* videowall presentation was also made possible through Appelt's generous support.

Pages 12-13: The quote is from page 12 of the book, *College Station Texas 1938/1988*, by Deborah McWilliams Balliew, College Station, Texas: Intaglio Press, 1987. The city of College Station, Texas is the home of Texas A&M University. Together with its sister city, Bryan, the area is commonly called the Brazos Valley, in reference to the Brazos River that runs nearby.

Pages 14-15: The *Here We'll Build the College* manuscript is held in the University Archives, which are located in Texas A&M's Cushing Memorial Library. Langford's quote appears on page 147. On page 146, Langford says, "to add further emphasis, sloped walks lead up to a promenade from which a long flight of steps leads to the main floor level. At that point fourteen freestanding modified Ionic columns set the scale of the building — a scale which is increased in height by a deep entablature and a third story."

According to an article by Lisa Nixon Sparks '81 entitled "Buildings Worth Remembering" that ran in the May 1981 issue of the *Texas Aggie* magazine (the alumni magazine of Texas A&M published by the Association of Former Students), "the fourteen pillars supporting the roof each have two faces on them. One face, resembling a Roman warrior, is Vosper's 'idealized portrait of the typical A&M cadet,' according to Langford. The other, the face of a young woman." Sparks also noted, "The front and back entrances feature men and women in romanticized agricultural situations, both on the doors themselves, and above the doors, in metal and masonry. The back entrances have peculiar columns between the doors, each featuring a medusa."

Pages 16-17: Patricia "Pat" Morley's quote is from a document she prepared for Texas A&M University dated April 5, 1983. It is held in the University Archives. Morley was longtime Administrative Assistant to Richard "Buck" Weirus '42, former Executive Director of the Association of Former Students. In the document, Morley notes that Carlos Marini supervised 100 stonemasons, who did the decorative cast stonework on what is now the Administration Building during the 1930s: "Carlos Marini immigrated from a city near Pisa [Italy]...had become renowned for his ornamental stonework...[was a] faithful Italian stone-master." Marini's daughter, Melba Marini Champion, stated that "coming to A&M has been...a wonderful experience for me...almost like a visit with my father."

The flagpole in front of the Administration Building is a gift from the Class of 1934.

Pages 18-19: The quote from Ernest Langford '13 appears on page 23 of his *Here We'll Build the College* manuscript.

The Oceanography and Meteorology Building, completed in 1972, was named in honor of David G. Eller '59 in 1988. Eller served as chairman of the Texas A&M University System Board of Regents from 1983 to 1989. The building is the tallest on the A&M campus.

Pages 20-21: The quote is from a letter that Lawrence Sullivan Ross wrote (on his first day as President of the A. & M. College) to his close friend, Major H.M. Holmes. In the letter, which is dated February 2, 1891, Ross states, "I have this morning assumed charge of the A. & M. C." The letter is held in the University Archives collection.

The campus of Texas A&M University spans over 5,200 acres, making it among the largest in the nation (source: TAMU Office of University Relations).

Pages 22-23: The quote from C.G. Forshey appears on page 40 in *History of the Agricultural and Mechanical College of Texas* by Clarence Ousley, published by the Agricultural and Mechanical College of Texas, College Station, Texas, in 1935.

On page 6 of *Here We'll Build the College*, Langford notes that "the three commissioners...apparently employed a Col. C.G. Forshey in some capacity even before the location of the college was determined." Col. Forshey signed himself as "Architect and Treasurer to the Commission" in a letter to Texas Governor E.J. Davis dated July 15, 1871. Langford further states, "it appears that he [Forshey] actually did work on the 'Drawings of the College.'"

Pages 24-25: The Association of Former Students building is named after Clayton W. Williams, Jr. '54, who provided a generous gift ensuring its completion. Williams was named a Distinguished Alumnus of Texas A&M in 1981.

Pages 26-27: The floral test gardens were created in 1969 as an idea of former A&M President Maj. Gen. James Earl Rudder '32. The gardens, which are maintained by the University's Horticultural Sciences Department, feature a variety of seasonal plantings.

James R. "Randy" Matson '67, quoted, has served as Executive Director of the Association of Former Students since 1980. An Olympic sports hero, Matson won silver and gold medals in the shot put during the 1960s. In Association publications, he describes its missions (from the official Association Charter): "to promote the interests and welfare of Texas A&M, to perpetuate the ties of friendships formed during college days, and to serve the student body by actively contributing to a climate of learning, tradition, and Aggie Spirit."

The 95-ton passive-flow fountain in front of the Alumni Center features a raised sculpture of the official seal of the Association of Former Students that was a gift of the Class of 1955. The fountain itself was dedicated in 1989 in memory of Henry A. Hansen '42 and in honor of his wife, Evelyn, by their three Aggie sons, Dr. H. Andrew Hansen II '71, Glenn E. Hansen '75, and Mark D. Hansen '79. An inscription on the fountain reads, "Real fathers are ordinary people with extraordinary love."

Pages 28-29: According to the Traditions Council at Texas A&M, the Aggie Ring is rich in symbolism and tradition. Seniors and graduates wear their class rings with pride. Unlike many universities, Texas A&M class rings may not be ordered until a student is a senior. The oldest known Aggie Ring dates back to the Class of 1889. The ring is worn with the class year facing the wearer, until he or she attends the annual Ring Dance, during which seniors turn their rings around to face the world.

The 60-inch Armillary Sphere is a sundial that displays the "sun time" for its precise location in College Station. It was donated by Searcy Bracewell '38, a Texas A&M Distinguished Alumnus.

Pages 30-31: The elegant home of the University President is located on campus among stately live oak trees on Throckmorton Street. It was completed in 1963 after the previous President's Home was destroyed by fire.

Pages 32-33: Texas A&M was the first public college founded in Texas, opening on October 4, 1876. Originally, it was an all-male military institution, but it is now fully coeducational and participation in its Corps of Cadets is voluntary (source: TAMU Office of University Relations).

The Corps Center opened in 1992 and is named after Sam Houston Sanders '22, who provided initial funding of a $1.5 million dollar donation toward its creation. In 1970, Sanders was admitted to the University's Athletic Hall of Fame and named a Distinguished Alumnus of Texas A&M. The Center features a brick plaza that displays names of individuals etched into bricks as memoriams or honorariums given by friends and family through a donation to a Center endowment. Corps cadets volunteer their time and energy to serve as official greeters and guides for the Center, according to *Cadence 1997*, a publication created for and given to Corps freshmen that explains many of the traditions and the history of Texas A&M.

The Corps of Cadets is the largest uniformed student organization in the nation (except for the service academies), with ROTC programs in all branches of the armed services. The all-voluntary organization comprises more than 2,100 members.

Margaret Segrest '94 said of Aggie traditions, "The essence of A&M traditions is unity. Texas A&M University brings students of varying backgrounds, cultures, and ethnicities together to be a part of something greater than themselves. Traditions that are rooted in loyalty and honor join over 43,000 students together, creating a community that acts very much like a large family."

Pages 34-35: The boots and hat pictured are only a small part of the vast collection of A&M memorabilia and research volumes housed in the Corps Center and its library. The diorama display in the center of the Great Hall is changed every few months. The Corps uniforms distinguish the approximately 2,100 Corps members from the other 41,000 or so students on campus — cadets wear their uniforms to every class, meal, and special event during the school year.

Pages 36-37: The case pictured contains football memorabilia, a history of the 12th Man, information about Aggie Yells and Yell Leaders, and more. The maroon yell leader sweater dates from 1959-60, the white sweater from 1922-23, and the autographed football from the 1939 National Championship season. The Book of Aggie Yells is circa 1922. Renowned football hero and 1957 Heisman Trophy winner John David Crow '58 was named the 1957 United Press International Back of the Year and a 1957 All-American.

Pages 38-39: The Sanders and Metzger Gun Collections display guns from "War Games, Seven Centuries to Revolving Rifles and Pepper Boxes," "War Between the States," "Guns of the West," "Muzzle Loaders," "Custom Guns," and the "Sam H. Sanders Commemorative Colt Collection" (which Sanders donated to the University). An ardent hunter, Carl Metzger donated one of the most complete exhibits of firearms in the world to the University. The 46-star flag previously hung in the bar of the Menger Hotel in San Antonio, Texas. It was reportedly used as a recruiting aid by Teddy Roosevelt when he was enlisting soldiers for the Spanish-American War. It is said to have traveled to Cuba and back with Teddy and the Rough Riders.

Pages 40-41: Marvin H. Mimms '26 wrote the lyrics to the "The Spirit of Aggieland" as a junior in 1925. Col. Richard J. Dunn, who retired from Texas A&M in 1946 after 22 years as bandmaster, wrote the music to the song, which is known as the University's *alma mater*. At the time of its composition, no college or university in the Southwest Conference had a school song with both original words and music.

One of the finest football facilities in the nation, Kyle Field is the home of the Fightin' Texas Aggie football team. It was named after Edwin Jackson Kyle, class of 1899, former Dean of Agriculture and President of the Athletic Council. Construction on the stadium began in 1927. With current expansions, it seats more than 80,000.

Pages 42-43: The bronze statue of the original 12th Man, E. King Gill '24, was crafted by George E. Foley and stands at the north end of Kyle Field. It was a gift of the Class of '80.

The 12th Man tradition is explained on the plaque at the base of the statue of Gill: "On January 2, 1922, Texas A&M played Centre College in the Dixie Classic in Dallas. After numerous injuries to the Aggie team, Coach Dana X. Bible called E. King Gill '24 from the stands. Gill, a basketball player and former football team member, suited up. He never entered the game, but his willingness to support the team provided inspiration for victory. The strong support of Aggies for their teams keeps alive that special part of the Aggie Spirit known as the Twelfth Man Tradition." Wording for the plaque was written by Jerry C. Cooper '63, Editor of the *Texas Aggie* magazine.

Photo of stadium by Jean Wulfson, TAMU Photo Imaging Services.

Pages 44-45: John David Crow '58 is quoted from a personal interview.

After many years in the Southwest Conference, the Texas A&M football team became a member of the "Big XII" Conference in 1996. The *College Journal* of February 1893 announced that A&M now "boasts a crack football team," according to page 10 of *Texas A&M University, A Pictorial History, 1876-1996*, by Henry C. Dethloff, second edition published by the Association of Former Students, Texas A&M University Press, College Station, Texas, 1996.

Yell Leaders are elected by the students after weeks of rigorous campaigning. Unlike most colleges and universities, which have "cheerleaders," Texas A&M has Yell Leaders, who lead members of the student body in traditional Aggie Yells at athletic events. The Yell Leaders conduct a series of Yell Practices to perfect these yells. Thousands of fans turn out for the practices, which are usually held at midnight the night prior to football games.

Goalpost photo by James Lyle, TAMU Photo Imaging Services. "Wrecking Crew" photo by Johnson Photography.

Pages 46-47: As Associate Director of the Fightin' Texas Aggie Band, Lt. Col. Jay O. Brewer '81 introduces the band's halftime performances at all A&M football games. "The best public relations firm could never conceive an idea that would add as much to the good name of this great institution as the Aggie Band," said H.C. "Dulie" Bell, Jr. '39 on April 13, 1973. Bell is quoted from his speech on behalf of the A&M Board of Directors at an appreciation dinner for Colonel E.V. Adams '29 in the *Texas Aggie* magazine article, "The 'Colonel' Steps Down," September 1973 issue. The campus Band Hall is named after the beloved Adams, who served 27 years (from 1946-1973) as bandmaster of the Aggie Band. A plaque in his honor says that Aggie bandsmen "stepped off for the 'Colonel' with a special marching magic that turned the heads and stirred the hearts of all who watched." Today's Fightin' Texas Aggie Band is composed of approximately 400 members, making it the world's largest military marching band.

"The Aggie War Hymn," which is A&M's fight song and the one that the Aggie Band "steps off to," was introduced as a school tradition in 1920. It was composed in 1918 in the trenches of France by J.V. "Pinky" Wilson '20. Wilson wrote the song as he stood guard on the Rhine following World War I. Another song commonly performed by the Aggie Band is "The Twelfth Man." Its lyrics and music were composed in 1941 by Lil (Mrs. Ford) Munnerlyn. She said, "to Texas Aggies everywhere, who, by their courage, loyalty and support, have made Aggie Spirit world-renowned, this song, 'The Twelfth Man,' is dedicated."

Photo of buglers by TAMU Photo Imaging Services. Photo of band on field by Barker Productions.

Pages 48-49: The Commandant of the Corps of Cadets, Maj. Gen. M.T. "Ted" Hopgood, Jr. '65, USMC (Ret.), is quoted addressing current members of the Corps in his composition, "Aggie Reflections." Members of the Texas A&M Corps of Cadets are known as the "Keepers of the Spirit."

The bronze statue pictured is one of three "Spirit of Bonfire" statues created in 1991 by Fred Adickes '52 that depict the Aggie Bonfire tradition. The group of statues was a gift from the Class of '87. According to *Cadence 1997*, "Before the annual football game with the University of Texas, Aggies build a huge bonfire, symbolizing their undying Aggie Spirit and the burning desire to beat the hell out of the rival school, affectionately known as t.u." Each year, Bonfire draws between 30,000 and 50,000 Aggie fans to celebrate and revel in its spirit. The Bonfire tradition began in the 1920s as a rally prior to the annual Texas A&M - University of Texas football game. The Bonfire stack then consisted of trash, boxes, and debris. The Bonfire, and the ceremonies and traditions surrounding it, have grown through the years, and today, hundreds of students — both "reg" (Corps) and "non-reg" (non-Corps) — join together to construct it. Chris Segrest '92, member of Company A-1, says, "One of the main reasons why Aggies are so unified behind their traditions is because of the Student Body's work on Bonfire." The Bonfire is the largest of its kind in the world. In the photo shown, according to Mark Ferrell, Class of 2000, Junior Centerpole Coordinator, "third and fourth stack tier ground men hoist rolls of wire used to secure the timbers up to their respective swing men."

Photo of suspended workers by Ryan Rogers, Class of 2000, *Battalion* newspaper. Photo of burning Bonfire by Mike Kellett '91, TAMU Photo Imaging Services.

Pages 50-51: The bronze Centennial Eagle by George E. Foley (1922-), is a stylized rendition of the University's centennial logo. Foley, whose son attended Texas A&M, also created the 12th Man statue.

The Victory Eagle is a bronze sculpture crafted by Kent Ullberg (1945-) of Corpus Christi, one of only two wildlife artists elected to the National Academy of Design in New York. The 1991 Class President said that the sculpture represents "the qualities that A&M instills in its graduates — strength, courage, and achievement."

Pages 52-53: According to its Constitution, the Parsons Mounted Cavalry "is a mounted military organization of volunteers…whose purpose is to attract attention to the University and its Corps of Cadets, recruit members for the Corps of Cadets, and demonstrate pride in the heritage and traditions of Texas A&M." The cadet pictured with his mount is Kevin Hebert, Class of 2000, who says that, as a member of the Cavalry, "you learn a lot about responsibility through the care of the horses." All members are required to take two equine classes. Mike Ogorchock, Class of 2000 (left), and Charles Gaitz '99 (right) are pictured at Cavalry Parents Weekend Review taking part in the tradition involving an incoming senior handing down his boot leggings to a junior. As is the case with other members of the Corps of Cadets, receiving one's coveted Senior Boots—which they will wear throughout their senior year at A&M— is a long-awaited and anticipated event. On his experience in the Cavalry, Ogorchock says that "looking back on the memories and the great friends I made and will keep for life, I wouldn't trade it for anything."

The Cavalry holds a review each Spring during Parents Weekend to recognize parents who support the organization.

Pages 54-55: The bugler (also pictured holding the flag) is James Lee Mutz, Jr., Class of 2000, who says that "being able to play songs like 'Reveille,' 'Taps,' or 'Assembly of Trumpeters' during functions such as march-ins, parades, or Final Review is the greatest honor I could possibly experience with the Cavalry." The Cavalry is named after Col. Thomas R. Parsons '49, who served as Commandant of Cadets when the Cavalry, originally founded in 1919, was revived in 1972 with a grant from the Association of Former Students.

Pages 56-57: The Ross Volunteers hold a review each Spring during Parents Weekend. Pictured reviewing them are Maj. Gen. M.T. "Ted" Hopgood, Jr. '65 and Maj. Greg Johnson '82. The Ross Volunteer Company is the oldest honor guard and drill team of its kind in the state. Founded in 1887 as the Scott Volunteers, they were eventually renamed in honor of Lawrence Sullivan Ross, former Governor of Texas. Ross accepted the presidency of the college in 1890, assumed office in 1891, and served as President until his death in 1898.

Pages 58-59: While Reveille belongs to the entire University, it is members of the Corps' Company E-2 who are charged with her care. Maj. Gen. Thomas Darling '54 says that "Reveille is a living symbol of the love, loyalty, and steadfast support that Aggies have for their school and each other." Company E-2 member Carlton Johnson, Class of 2000, notes that Reveille marches in front of the Company for military reviews, march-ins, or whenever the outfit is in block formation. She attends all A&M football games, at home or away.

Pages 60-61: John Ashton '06 wrote "Good-Bye, Reveille" as a tribute to the first Aggie mascot (Reveille I) after her death in 1944. Every Reveille is given a military funeral at Kyle Field.

Company E-2 member Eddie LeBlanc, Class of 2001 (pictured cleaning the gravestone plaque) says that "to most people, Reveille is the Fightin' Texas Aggie mascot; to us, she is the cornerstone of our pride." The tradition of the Aggie mascot began many years ago when several cadets picked up a black and white puppy. Against regulations, the cadets brought the puppy back to sleep with them in the dormitory. When reveille sounded the next morning, the dog howled in disapproval, and she was known from then on as Reveille. She soon had free run of campus, and debuted as the official A&M mascot by leading the Aggie Band onto the field at the 1931 A&M-Texas game.

Pages 62-63: Pictured at Muster 1998 is Heather Teel '99, who says that the meaningful "Muster experience is unexplainable, yet every person involved leaves with a deeper understanding of the Aggie Spirit." Heather holds a candle during the solemn ceremony in which she answers "here" for a fallen Aggie.

According to the Campus Muster program, April 21, 1998, Roll Call for the Absent was first held in 1883, when Aggies met on June 26 to "live over again our college days, the victories and defeats won and lost upon the drill field and classroom." In the early 1900s it was agreed that, in addition to honoring the freedom of Texas, April 21 would be a good time to pay homage to all students and former students who have passed on, and that some living comrade would answer "here" when the roll call for the absent was read. "Let every alumnus answer a roll call," wrote the former students, then known as ex-cadets. During World War I, Aggies met in foxholes all over Europe and at Army posts in America, but no Musters were held on campus during that time.

In 1942, Muster gained national recognition when it was reported that Aggie soldiers gathered on Corregidor Island in the Philippines. Fifteen days before the island fell, 25 men, led by Gen. George Moore '08, "mustered in the dim recesses of the rock and answered 'here' for their dead classmates." And so it has been over the years, becoming one of Texas A&M's greatest traditions. Muster is more than just a ceremony. It is a way for Aggies to renew each year the loyalty and unity that constitute the foundation of their friendship for each other and their love and devotion for the school.

Today, Aggie Muster is held in over 400 locations worldwide, traditionally on April 21. The largest Muster ceremony is held on the A&M campus in the Reed Arena. Past Musters have featured noteworthy speakers, including General Dwight Eisenhower.

Photo of Muster by TAMU Photo Imaging Services. Photo of Heather Teel '99 holding candle by Ryan Rogers, Class of 2000, *Battalion* newspaper.

Pages 64-65: The quote from Governor Richard Coke was from his address at the A&M College of Texas dedication ceremony, October 4, 1876. Coke's address is held in the University Archives.

All cadets participate in Corps Final Review, which is held each year in May. Pictured are (foreground) Corps Commander Tyson T. Voelkel '96 and (to his left) Regiment Commander Laurent C. Therivel '96. Voelkel says that, at the ceremony, "Seniors proudly look on to those fish, sophomores, and juniors, knowing that they helped create the future leaders of the Corps, the University, and invariably, our nation." Laurent Therivel says that the ceremony is "all about the Company — the family. You stand on the field swaying to 'The Aggie War Hymn' for the last time as a Corps member. You're so proud, not of yourself, but of this organization that you helped mold and that you see saluting you for the last time."

Photo of Final Review by James Lyle, TAMU Photo Imaging Services.

Pages 66-67: The names of 916 Aggies who died during World War II are inscribed on bronze tablets at the main entrance of the Memorial Student Center. Another plaque honors 104 Aggies "who led and supported us during the gallant defense of Bataan and Corregidor from 8 December 1941 to 6 May 1942." On the pillars of the MSC's north corridor hang portraits of Texas A&M's seven recipients of the Congressional Medal of Honor.

Pages 68-69: The quote about Tent Row appears on page 87 of *Here We'll Build the College*, a manuscript held in the University Archives. It also states that in an area of about 10 acres "are stretched 243 tents."

Noted architecture professor Rodney C. Hill was commissioned to design and carve the 100-year history of Texas A&M University, and spent four months researching, interviewing, and reviewing documents, artifacts, and photographs for the wood panels that line an interior wall of the Memorial Student Center. Rodney's wife, Sue Hill, who contributed to the project, said that becoming "a part of that history is a thrill that never goes away. It was a humbling experience to realize the enormity of Texas A&M with the university's involvement in virtually every aspect of life relating to land, sea, and space."

Pages 70-71: Maj. Gen. James Earl Rudder '32 served as President of Texas A&M University from 1959 until his death in 1970. He also served as President of the A&M System from 1965 until 1970. Rudder was instrumental in setting Texas A&M on its path to becoming the great university that it is today. He was named a Distinguished Alumnus in 1970.

Rudder was a military hero: during the D-day assault in World War II, he lead his "Rudder's Rangers" up the cliffs at Pointe du Hoc, France, against German resistance. According to Mrs. Margaret Rudder (his widow), General Rudder was given command on December 8, 1944 of the 109th Regiment of the 28th Infantry Division, which is credited with blunting the German attack in the Battle of the Bulge. Rudder later served as Mayor of Brady, Texas, and as Commissioner of the General Land Office of Texas. Richard Conolly '37 said that "few men ever lived who could have done what he accomplished in a few short years." Conolly worked with Frank Muller '65 to obtain private donations to pay for the statue of Rudder.

The statue was sculpted by Houston artist Lawrence Ludtke. Passing the statue is Sergio Flores '98, who states, "I would have never forgiven myself had I not joined the Corps. The Fightin' Texas Aggie Band introduced me to the best friends of my life. They will marry me and bury me."

Pages 72-73: Danny Breed '99 admires a portrait of General Rudder painted by J. Anthony Wills and a collection of Rudder's military medals and honors.

Texas A&M University's Memorial Student Center Opera and Performing Arts Society (MSC OPAS) was founded in 1972 as a vehicle to support the arts in the community by bringing cultural presentations to such venues as the Rudder Theater Complex, which opened the following year. Members of the local community and the university community, including a large number of enthusiastic student volunteers, work together each season to bring outstanding programs to campus. Over the years, internationally-renowned artists such as Van Cliburn, Itzhak Perlman, Rudolf Nureyev, the cast of CATS, and the Bolshoi Ballet Grigorovich Company have performed at Rudder Auditorium under the auspices of MSC OPAS. The venue is also used for other events such as Brazos Valley Symphony performances.

The ballet photo by Larissa Pedenchuk is provided courtesy of Columbia Artists Management Inc., New York, NY.

Pages 74-75: The Forsyth Center Galleries, located in the Memorial Student Center, offer a rich collection of fine and decorative arts. As the home of the Bill ('35) & Irma Runyon Art Collections, the Galleries house one of the world's most extraordinary collections of English Cameo Glass, as well as 1100 American and English glass objects and 66 American paintings. The Painting Collections include important works by Mary Cassatt, Frederic Remington, and Charles M. Russell. The Glass Collections include the masterful works of Louis Comfort Tiffany, Steuben Glass Works, the New England and Mount Washington Glass Companies, and long-term loans of Gallé and American rich cut glass.

Mr. Runyon's commitment to the students of Texas A&M University was that they would have access to the finest original art available. It was equally important to him that the Galleries would be inviting, informative, and stimulating. The Runyon Collections include paintings, watercolors, and drawings.

All objects courtesy of MSC Forsyth Center Galleries, Bill and Irma Runyon Art Collections, Texas A&M Foundation (photo of gallery interior by Bob Herger).

Pages 76-77: The Stark Galleries host about 14 traveling exhibitions a year, with offerings ranging from traditional fine arts and crafts to anthropology, archaeology, history, and science. The permanent collection includes works by a number of acclaimed Texas artists.

J. Wayne Stark '39 (1915-1993) was the founding director of the Memorial Student Center. He was passionate about bringing museum-quality art into the immediate environment of Texas A&M students. He founded the University Art Collection, created and nurtured the MSC Visual Arts Committee, and established the University Art Exhibits program. He organized the Texas A&M Commission on the Visual Arts, which provided impetus to build the galleries.

Charles Schorre's quote appears on page 155 of *Charles Schorre* by Jerry Herring, published by Herring Press and the Houston Artists Fund, 1997. "Touchrush," the prominently displayed painting from the Schorre exhibit, was on loan to the galleries from the collection of Betty and Frederic Fleming.

Ivana Candiago's Polyopsia exhibition in the Visual Arts Gallery (Spring 1998) is representative of the outstanding quality of temporary exhibits on display in each of the galleries.

The Memorial Student Center also houses the L.T. Jordan Institute for International Awareness Collection.

Pages 78-79: The Cushing Memorial Library re-opened in 1998 after extensive renovation. It houses rare books, special collections, manuscripts, and the official University Archives collection. It is named for Col. E.B. Cushing (Class of 1880), who is quoted from a letter he wrote to a cadet. The letter appeared in *The Reveille* December 7, 1918, and is held in the University Archives. Cushing is best-known for "saving" the University during a time of financial woe. In 1912, when the Texas Legislature threatened to close A&M and move it to Austin as part of the University of Texas, Cushing personally guaranteed notes of credit for the college.

Cushing served in numerous leadership capacities on behalf of the college, including service as President of the A&M Board of Directors from 1912 to 1915. According to page 170 of *A Centennial History of Texas A&M University*

by Henry C. Dethloff (published by the Association of Former Students, Texas A&M University Press, College Station, Texas, 1975), Cushing sponsored Alpha Phi (forerunner of the The Association of Former Students) and served several terms as President. He was reportedly "one of the finest heads the Association has ever had," according to a July 21, 1948 *Battalion* article by Chuck Maisel '49, entitled, "Life of Cushing Reads Like History of College He Loved," which is held in the University Archives.

In a January 10, 1961 letter (also held in the Archives), R.H. Shuffler '29 wrote, "E.B. Cushing acquired the title of Colonel in World War I...on the staff of General Pershing. He received a number of decorations, including the French Legion of Honor."

The Dunton painting was a gift from the family of James L. Marr; the Corrodi painting was a gift of C.C. "Polly" Krueger '12; and the purchase of the Shakespeare folio was made possible through a gift from Chester J. Reed '47.

Photos of art and literature pieces provided courtesy of the Cushing Memorial Library, Texas A&M University. Photo of the library by David O. Cooper.

Pages 80-81: The Bible quote is inscribed on the Memorial Student Center at the entrance, above the names of Aggies killed in World War II. The Fish Pond fountain, a familiar landmark on the A&M campus, was presented by the Class of 1938 to honor twelve classmates who were killed during World War II.

Pages 82-83: According to *Footsteps, a Guided Tour of the Texas A&M University Campus* by Jerry C. Cooper '63 and Henry C. Dethloff (Texas A&M University Press, 1991), "construction on the Academic Building began in 1912, literally on the ashes of Old Main, the first building constructed at A&M, which had burned to the ground the previous year. The new building was designed by Samuel E. Gideon, at the time an instructor in architecture, and built by Frederick Ernst Giesecke (Class of 1886), a professor of civil engineering."

According to Ernest Langford on page 94 of *Here We'll Build the College*, "The Academic Building may be described as being 'right out of the books'...a classicist to the very soles of his feet, Mr. Gideon went to the Ecole des Beaux-Arts for his inspiration." Langford noted that the building "has stood as a symbol of the academic life of Texas A&M College."

Pages 84-85: The Honorable Norman G. Kittrell was a Houston judge. The quote is from page 86 of the book, *Second Five Administrators of Texas A. & M. College 1890-1905* by David Brooks Cofer, copyright 1954 by the Association of Former Students of Texas A. and M. College.

Silver Taps is a ceremony held on campus to pay tribute to those who have died while enrolled as students at Texas A&M. It is held on the first Tuesday of each month at 10:30 p.m. in front of the Academic Building, where the flag is flown at half-mast. As they do at Muster ceremonies, the Corps' Ross Volunteers perform their 21-gun salute at Silver Taps. Six buglers play the song, "Silver Taps," three times—to the north, west, and south. The first Silver Taps ceremony was held in 1898 for Lawrence Sullivan Ross upon his death.

The bronze Silver Taps monument, a gift from the Class of 1991, was created by A&M architecture professor Rodney C. Hill, and is located in the circular planting bed near the flagpole on Military Walk. An inscription on the monument explains the Silver Taps tradition to passers-by.

Pages 86-87: On January 4th, 1898, the *Galveston Daily News* published a glowing article about Lawrence Sullivan Ross, from which the quote is taken. A copy of the article is held in the University Archives. Ross was a former Texas Governor and beloved President of the University, then known as the A. & M. College.

The bronze sculpture of Ross was crafted by Pompeo Coppini (1870-1957) in 1918. In a letter to the University dated April 5, 1983, Patricia "Pat" Morley said, "Pompeo Coppini has many statues of Texas heroes enshrined in the Capitol—but perhaps none as frequently washed or shined as his beloved statue at A&M, affectionately known as Sully."

Pages 88-89: According to Ernest Langford in *Here We'll Build the College* (1963), page 96, "The rotunda of the building is framed by twenty poured-in-place reinforced concrete columns in each floor. Those of the lower floor are plain Doric; those of the upper floors are also Doric but fluted. The columns are arranged in groups of five around a circle about thirty-six feet in diameter."

According to *Footsteps*, "The Liberty Bell replica, suspended at the second floor level under the rotunda, was given to the State of Texas in 1950 as part of a U.S. Savings Bond drive sponsored by private industry. Gov. Allan Shivers, in turn, presented it to Texas A&M in recognition of the sacrifices made by Aggies in the defense of the nation. Under the bell is a fourteen-foot-diameter mosaic of the university seal, the work of Joseph M. Hutchinson, an A&M professor of architecture. A gift of the Class of 1978, it originally contained 36,000 tiles."

The Albritton Tower is a gift of Martha and Ford D. Albritton, Jr. '43.

Pages 90-91: Ford D. Albritton, Jr. '43 is a Distinguished Alumnus of Texas A&M, past President of the Association of Former Students, and former member of the Texas A&M University System Board of Regents. At the tower dedication ceremonies on October 6, 1984, Albritton spoke fondly of Texas A&M, saying, "It was here I learned the principles of leadership," according to the December 1984 *Texas Aggie* magazine article, "Albritton Tower: A New A&M Landmark." The tower stands 138 feet high and contains a 49-bell carillon. The bells, which ring every quarter hour and on special occasions, have a total combined weight of some 34,000 pounds.

The college was established when an act of the Texas Legislature was approved on April 17, 1871. According to Henry C. Dethloff's *A Centennial History of Texas A&M University* (pg. 19), "...the people of Bryan energetically worked for the location of the college...they made a substantial gift to the college, and...it was located near the population center of the state and along a railroad which provided, for the time, excellent transportation."

In June 1915, Austin E. Burges stated, in his published local history of the Agricultural and Mechanical College of Texas, "through the agency of Colonel Harvey Mitchell...the Commission awarded the location of the College to Brazos County." Burges' account was included in Clarence Ousley's *History of the Agricultural and Mechanical College of Texas.*

Pages 92-93: The bronze sculpture of Robert Justus Kleberg, Jr. was donated by Mrs. Helen Groves and the Kleberg family. It was crafted by renowned Western artist Jim Reno (1929-) in 1983. Reno is famous for his portraits of horses that have won the Kentucky Derby. He said the statue represents the character of an individual who helped to win the West. Kleberg owned and directed the King Ranch for over 30 years. He did much to support Texas A&M as well as contributing to the Texas cattle and livestock industry. Kleberg received an honorary degree in agriculture from Texas A&M in 1941.

Pages 94-95: The quote from Governor Richard Coke was from his October 4, 1876 address at the A&M College of Texas dedication ceremony. Coke's address is held in the University Archives.

The Koldus Building is a modern building with classical elements. It is made of brick with cast stone detailing, and features terrazzo flooring, most evident in the colorful mosaic University seal inlaid in the main foyer floor.

The Roughneck bronze sculpture, crafted by Rosie Sandifer in 1991, was a gift of Mrs. Susan Richardson. It was commissioned to commemorate the dedication of the petroleum engineering building, the Richardson Building, which is named after Joe C. Richardson, Jr. '49, an independent oil and gas operator from Amarillo. Richardson served on the Texas A&M University System Board of Regents and was named a Distinguished Alumnus in 1989.

Pages 96-97: The quote is from a letter dated August 8, 1890, that Governor Lawrence Sullivan Ross wrote upon accepting the presidency of the college. In emphasizing the importance of exercise, he was referencing the benefits of physical discipline that military life at the college instills.

The Texas A&M Student Recreation Center opened in 1995 as a premier recreational sports facility. It features 373,000 square feet of recreational space that includes a 42-foot 3-dimensional indoor rock climbing structure; a natatorium with a 50-meter, 8-lane Olympic-size pool, an instructional pool, and a diving well with spring boards and competitive platforms; and multi-purpose gyms and courts.

The Reed Arena, completed in 1998, seats 12,500 for concerts, family entertainment, athletic events, and more. The impressive arena floor measures 25,000 square feet. It is the home of the A&M men's and women's basketball

teams. The building is named in honor of Chester J. Reed '47, a Distinguished Alumnus of Texas A&M.

Pages 98-99: The abstract steel sculpture called "Rapport" is inspired by the quote, "Nature is the handmaiden of healing." It was created by Joseph Smith (1921-) and Ben Woitena (1942-) in 1993. It depicts a human figure with outstretched arms.

Medical students in the Texas A&M University System Health Science Center College of Medicine spend their first two years studying in College Station, and then relocate to complete their studies at hospitals and clinics affiliated with the college, which include Scott & White Memorial Hospital in Temple, Texas.

Pages 100-101: The quote from Col. E.B. Cushing was from his letter to a cadet dated October 10, 1918. The letter is held in the University Archives.

The Association of Former Students' membership exceeds 200,000. It is dedicated to serving former students and the University (including its current students, faculty, and staff). Association support includes raising millions of dollars for student scholarships and University programs and facilities; sponsoring and supporting more than 200 A&M Clubs and 340 Aggie Musters all over the world; coordinating class reunions; and operating the Aggie Ring Office.

Pages 102-103: George Bush spoke about character during a lecture on presidential rhetoric that he delivered to graduate students at Texas A&M in 1996 (source: article about the Bush School of Government and Public Service by Laura Kurk that appeared in the Texas A&M University System newsletter, "A&M System, Texas," September 1997 issue).

A host of friends, celebrities, and dignitaries came to the Texas A&M campus when the George Bush Presidential Library and Museum opened in November 1997. In addition to President Bush and more than 60 family members, President Bill Clinton and First Lady Hillary Rodham Clinton attended, as did Presidents Jimmy Carter and Gerald Ford and their wives. First Ladies Nancy Reagan and Lady Bird Johnson also attended.

The Library and Museum chronicle the life of President Bush, including his private life and career since the end of his presidency in 1993. Nearly 40 million documents and 1 million photographs are catalogued in Library archives. Noteworthy displays and exhibits include a duplicate of the World War II plane that Bush flew as the youngest pilot in the Navy; a replica of his offices at Camp David and aboard Air Force One; and a bronze sculpture located outside the Library celebrating the fall of the Berlin Wall. The Museum contains approximately 60,000 historical objects, including unique Head of State gifts, as well as gifts from the American people.

Pages 104-105: The quote from George Bush is from his remarks at the groundbreaking of the Presidential Library Complex.

The George Bush School of Government and Public Service opened September 10, 1997, in the Presidential Library Complex. The school is dedicated to training future public servants by offering a Master of Public Service and Administration degree. Bush is actively involved with the school and visits frequently to deliver lectures to students.

The Bush Library Complex also includes the Presidential Conference Center, which offers meeting rooms and auditorium facilities for Library activities and special events sponsored by the University.

Pages 106-107: General Rudder's remarks from his Muster Address on April 21, 1956, are held in the Texas A&M University Archives.

Carved in limestone on the east face of the Presidential Library and Museum are these words:

"LET FUTURE GENERATIONS UNDERSTAND THE BURDEN AND THE BLESSINGS OF FREEDOM.

LET THEM SAY WE STOOD WHERE DUTY REQUIRED US TO STAND."

PRESIDENT GEORGE BUSH, JANUARY, 1991